Ancient
China

Archaeology Unlocks the Secrets of China's Past

By Jacqueline Ball and Richard Levey

Robert Murowchick, Consultant

NATIONAL
GEOGRAPHIC
Washington, DC

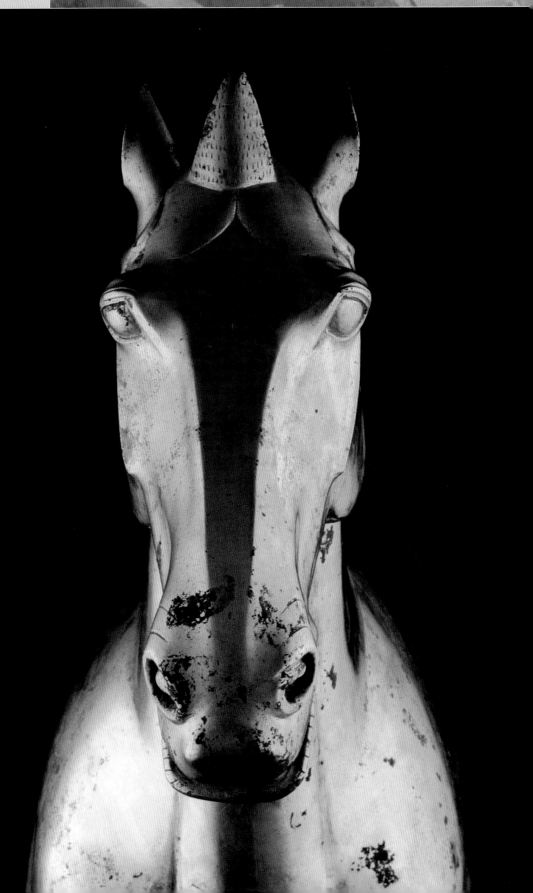

Contents

Message From the Authors 8

Map of Important Archaeological Sites in China 9

Maps of Three Major Chinese Dynasties 10-11

Timeline of Chinese History 10-11

Yesterday Comes Alive
12-17

Oral tradition • Written history • Artifacts • Archaeology may confirm the historical record • How archaeologists do their work • Using timelines • Focus on the Shang, Qin, and Han dynasties

Tales Told by Turtles
18-25

Zheng Zhenxiang • Discovering a tomb • Oracle bones • Contextual dating • Messages on turtle shells • Fu Hao • Radiocarbon dating • Inside Fu Hao's tomb • Meet an archaeologist

A Silent Army
26-33

Finding the terra-cotta warriors • Qin Shi Huangdi's tomb • No two warriors alike • Ying Zheng becomes Qin Shi Huangdi • Source of the name "China" • The Great Wall of China • Pollution and moisture threaten the warriors • Ground-penetrating radar

Dressed for Success
34-39

Liu Sheng and Dou Wan • Jade burial suits • Magical properties of jade • Silk as a state secret

< A gilded bronze horse, thought to be a gift from an emperor to his sister, reflects the prosperity of the Han dynasty.

5 Learn from Your Mummy   40-45

Changsha • Xin Zhui, Lady Dai • Lady Dai's autopsy •
The tomb of Lady Dai • Desert mummies • Lady
Dai's secret

6 Good Job, Goodbye!   46-53

Royal tombs contain clues about the lives of ordinary
people • Building tombs • Human and animal sacrifice •
"Following in death" • Grave goods and the afterlife •
The Neolithic Age • China's Bronze Age • Erlitou

7 Tomb Robbers!   54-57

Tomb robbers • Looted artifacts • Empress Dou •
Government measures to stop tomb robberies •
Damage done by tomb robbers • Looting destroys
the ancient record

The Years Ahead	58
Glossary	59
Bibliography	60
Further Reading and Information	60
Web Sites	60
Index	61-62
About the Authors and Consultant	63
Credits	64

◀ A portion of the Great Wall of China, interrupted by numerous watchtowers

We are not scientists, but we are interested in scientific ideas. Because we also like reading about history, books about archaeology capture our interest right away. We find it astonishing how much is known about ancient China and the lives of the people who lived there so long ago. We think archaeologists are amazing as they patiently put together clues from the past, bit by bit, opening a window to days gone by. We learned a lot working with Dr. Robert Murowchick on this book.

It's especially exciting to have an opportunity to share our enthusiasm about archaeology with an audience of young readers. You may have thought that archaeology would be dry and dusty and boring. Nothing could be farther from the truth! Archaeologists have incredible adventures, often risking danger to get the answers they seek. And the science of archaeology is not at all old-fashioned. Archaeologists use the latest in technology to help them uncover the wonders of the past. Depending on the people they are studying, archaeologists may work at high altitudes, atop mountains. Or they may dive deep underwater to study sunken sites.

We invite you to turn the page, and do some digging of your own, discovering the secrets of China's past.

-Jacqueline Ball and Richard Levey

> Measuring 8½ feet (2.6 m) tall, this magnificent bronze sculpture of a human figure is from the time period of the Shang dynasty. But its relationship to the Shang culture is much debated.

>> Archaeologist and consultant Robert Murowchick and his colleagues discuss excavation results at a Neolithic village site in eastern China.

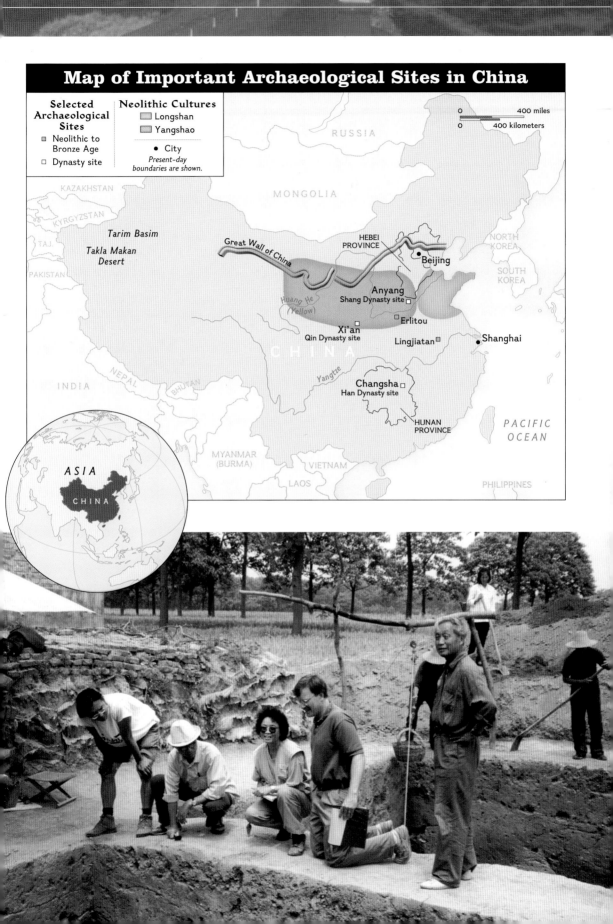

Map of Important Archaeological Sites in China

Selected Archaeological Sites
- ▣ Neolithic to Bronze Age
- ▢ Dynasty site

Neolithic Cultures
- ▨ Longshan
- ▨ Yangshao

● City

Present-day boundaries are shown.

0 ____ 400 miles
0 ____ 400 kilometers

RUSSIA

MONGOLIA

KAZAKHSTAN

KYRGYZSTAN

TAJ.

PAKISTAN

Tarim Basim

Takla Makan Desert

Great Wall of China

HEBEI PROVINCE

● Beijing

NORTH KOREA

SOUTH KOREA

Anyang
Shang Dynasty site ▢

Huang He (Yellow)

Xi'an ▢
Qin Dynasty site

Erlitou ▢

Lingjiatan ▢

● Shanghai

C H I N A

NEPAL

BHUTAN

INDIA

Yangtze

Changsha ▢
Han Dynasty site

HUNAN PROVINCE

PACIFIC OCEAN

MYANMAR (BURMA)

VIETNAM

LAOS

PHILIPPINES

ASIA

CHINA

Shang Dynasty

circa 1600 – 1045 B.C.

The wealthy, powerful Shang culture ruled over the North China Plain during China's Bronze Age (ca. 1600-400 B.C.). Bronze weapons and ritual vessels, as well as beautiful jade and ivory objects, have been found at the site of the last Shang capital city near modern Anyang. Writings on oracle bones from Anyang give important clues to religious practices and daily life.

Shang

Qin Dynasty

221 – 206 B.C.

In 221, a man named Ying Zheng conquered all the Chinese states. He unified them under himself and took the title Shi Huangdi, or "First Emperor." This started the Qin dynasty and China's imperial period. "China" comes from the word "Qin."

Under Qin rule, a major portion of the Great Wall was completed. Writing, weights and measures, and coins were standardized.

< A heavily detailed Shang sculpture of a tiger with a bird on its back

Timeline of Chinese History

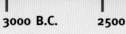

3000 B.C.	2500	2000	1500	1000	500	
		Xia (?)				Han
NEOLITHIC CULTURES		circa 2000 B.C.	Shang	Zhou		206
Yangshao–circa 5000-3000 B.C.			circa 1600	circa 1045		
Liangzhu–circa 3300-2200 B.C.						Qin
Longshan–circa 3000-2000 B.C.						221

Bronze Age
China

◁ A horned, tongue-wagging face made from terra-cotta was used to ward off evil in Han times.

Han Dynasty

206 B.C. — A.D. 220

A peasant named Liu Bang led a revolt that brought down the last Qin ruler and became the first Han emperor. During the Han dynasty, China expanded into present-day Korea, Vietnam, and Central Asia. Trade between China and the West opened up. Chinese silk appeared in the Roman Empire for the first time, brought by caravans on the Silk Road.

Qin

Han

▷ Helmets made of limestone plates connected by bronze thread were excavated at the tomb complex of Qin Shi Huangdi.

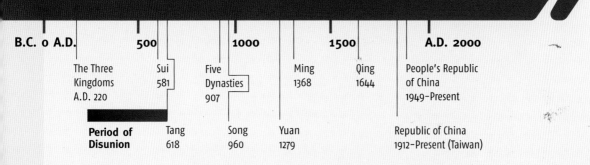

B.C. 0 A.D.	500	1000	1500	A.D. 2000
The Three Kingdoms A.D. 220	Sui 581	Five Dynasties 907	Ming 1368	Qing 1644	People's Republic of China 1949–Present

Period of Disunion — Tang 618 — Song 960 — Yuan 1279 — Republic of China 1912–Present (Taiwan)

Yesterday Comes Alive

CHAPTER 1

How do we learn what we know about the past?

Information can come to us in a number of ways. Sometimes people have an oral tradition— they pass stories about their past from generation to generation through the spoken word. It's hard for us to learn about history this way, unless people who still know the old stories are alive. Other times, people may have a written history, and by studying what has been written down, we can learn about their lives. Don't be fooled into thinking that written history is just in books, written on paper. History may be carved on a stone tablet or painted on a tomb wall.

< Workers take samples of earth from an area within the tomb complex of Qin Shi Huangdi, whose burial mound rises in the background.

Historians study all forms of written history, piecing bits together to form a picture of the past.

There is a third way to learn about people from the past, and that is what this book is about. *Archaeologists* are scientists who study the objects—called *artifacts*— that people have left behind, the sites where these are found, and the landscapes in which the site existed. These artifacts give us clues about how people lived their lives in earlier times. The artifacts may be scattered, discovered one at a time. Or they may be together, in a place where a village or settlement once stood. This book focuses mostly on artifacts—including skeletons and mummies—found in old tombs.

All of the information archaeologists discover can be compared to the written history and the oral history we know about. Sometimes archaeology confirms the historical record. The discovery of Liu Sheng's jade suit described in chapter 4 proved that earlier writings describing such suits were true. But sometimes what archaeologists find raises new questions about the things we think we know about people from the past.

Regardless of what they find, archaeologists keep very careful records of the site when a discovery is made, drawing or photographing artifacts in place before removing them for further study. As you'll read in chapter 2, the archaeologists who

yanked things out of Fu Hao's tomb were breaking all the rules, because of rapidly rising water. They were afraid of losing what they had just found!

Just how do archaeologists decide where to look for evidence of the past? Sometimes studying written and oral history points them in the right direction. Other times they study

∧ Core samples are taken from a pit in the tomb complex of the First Emperor of Qin.

> An incense burner, or "vast mountain brazier," unearthed from a royal Han tomb shows a figure atop a dragon, and had important religious meaning.

landforms in a certain region, looking for caves or hills where artifacts may be hidden or buried. And sometimes, the discovery of a ruin or tomb is a happy accident, the result of digging a well or building a shopping center!

The tools archaeologists use range from very simple to very complicated. Ordinary shovels and brushes may help them to uncover artifacts from the past, carefully cleaning away the dirt that has kept them hidden. Screens are used to sift dirt, so that even the tiniest artifact will not be

<An assassin lunges at the emperor Qin Shi Huangdi. The attacker had come as a friend, bearing the head of a slain enemy in a box, while concealing his dagger in a rolled map. The emperor draws his own weapon while he leaps behind a column.

Historians and archaeologists have used timelines like the one on pages 10–11 for many years, in an attempt to organize the various periods of Chinese history. Such a timeline shows history with one thing happening after another, step-by-step. In reality, however, the story of the past is not that simple. Different groups of people may or may not interact with each other. Groups may be isolated from each other, existing at the same time but in different locations, with no knowledge of each other. Or they might overlap, interacting with each other through trade or marriage, changing each other along the way.

The simple timeline shown in this book will help to give you a general understanding as you read about ancient China, basically the time period from 2000 B.C. to A.D. 1279. Within that time frame, we'll be focusing on three major periods of Chinese history: the Shang, Qin, and Han dynasties.

The history of ancient China becomes richer and more complex with each new archaeological discovery. Something uncovered tomorrow may change everything we think we know today.

lost. But these days, increasingly technological methods are used in archaeology. You'll read about ground-penetrating radar in chapter 4. Even satellites can be put to work to help locate underground ruins that are not clearly visible from the surface of the Earth.

Tales Told by Turtles

What do old turtle shells with mysterious carvings tell us about China's ancient past?

In 1976, archaeologists uncovered several royal burial tombs from Shang-dynasty China, which began nearly 4,000 years ago around 1600 B.C. Tombs are wonderful for archaeologists because their contents can tell us a lot about how the person or people buried there lived. But

< Archaeologists excavate tombs in a Shang cemetery at Anyang.

SHANG DYNASTY
circa 1600 - 1045 B.C.

1500   1000   500   B.C. 0 A.D. 300

these tombs had been looted by tomb robbers and were empty. They could not tell their stories.

One archaeologist, Zheng Zhenxiang, now with the Chinese Academy of Social Sciences, was sure there was another tomb in a particular spot outside the city. Zheng and her team dug there. They had found the tomb! Suddenly their spades pushed below water level, and freezing water rushed in, opening up the pit and rising to their waists. Over time, the archaeologists would bring up bronze weapons, jade statues, bone necklaces—and human skeletons.

Whose Tomb?

Zheng and her team saved as many objects as they could quickly. Then they worked to learn as much as possi-

∧ This bronze head is also from the Shang period, but archaeologists debate its connection to Shang culture.

ble about what they had found. They worked carefully, charting, cleaning, and analyzing their finds.

The tomb is a single large pit about 18 feet (5.6 m) by 13 feet (4 m). In a small hole beneath the main floor of the pit, archaeologists found the remains of six dogs. Sixteen human skeletons lay around the edges of the tomb. It looked as if the dogs and humans had been left to guard the owner of the tomb in the afterlife.

About 2,000 items were found in the tomb, including bronze weapons, bells, knives, and ritual vessels for holding food and wine. There were 750 jade necklaces and statues, hundreds of arrowheads, bone hairpins and carved ivory items, and nearly 7,000 cowry shells, which were used for money across much of Asia during the Shang dynasty.

The coffin in the center of the tomb had rotted and the skeleton of

∧ During the Shang dynasty, artisans created beautiful bronze vessels like this one.

the tomb owner was completely disintegrated. Who was this person?

The archaeologists hoped that the contents of the tomb would help them to identify its owner.

Oracle Bones

For much of what we know about ancient China, we can thank turtles. At least, we can thank their shells. Messages on turtle shells from ancient tombs have helped bring ancient China to life. These ancient writings are called *oracle bones*.

Oracle means "vision" or "prediction." In the Shang culture, oracle bones were used to predict the future. A ruler or a priest called a *shaman* heated a turtle shell, a tortoise shell, or even the shoulder blade of an ox until it cracked. The patterns of the

Contextual Dating

Millet

Archaeologists found a grain called *millet* near the bones of a Shang-dynasty skeleton. Contextual dating—determining the age of an artifact from an unknown period because it is found near items that have been linked to a specific period—indicated that the grain was probably from the Shang dynasty, too. But it would take radio-carbon dating (see page 23) to prove that that was true.

> Rulers or priests used ox bones (front) and turtle shells (background) to communicate with the spirit world.

cracks were believed to be messages from the spirit world—predictions from dead ancestors or the gods who controlled the sun, the rain, and human life.

But the shamans of Anyang were special. Sometimes an Anyang shaman would carve a question on the shell or bone before heating it. After it cracked, the shaman carved his or her translation of the cracks into the oracle bone along with the question.

Archaeologists working in tombs around Anyang earlier had found oracle bones with questions about the future of someone named Fu Hao. The word *Fu* was a royal title, like the title "Lady" in medieval Europe, so the name alone told the archaeologists that Fu Hao was an important woman. There were questions about her health, about how the birth of her child would go, and also about battles

∨ This wine vessel, called a gong, was found in the tomb of Lady Hao.

band war. One oracle bone revealed that the king himself had assembled soldiers to fight in Fu Hao's army. This Fu Hao was not a typical woman of her time. She was a military leader.

So when Zheng's team were excavating the new tomb, they were thrilled to find bronze items with the name of Fu Hao on them. They came to the conclusion that their skeleton and the woman of the oracle bones were one and the same person.

Fu Hao

Life was good for Fu Hao during the ancient Chinese Shang dynasty. She had plenty of money in the form of cowry shells, and she wore necklaces of the finest handworked jade. Her hair was held back with exquisitely carved bone pins. Her clothing was made of the softest silk. Attendants served her food from a *ding*, a pot made of bronze that stood on three legs. She ate wheat or a grain called *millet*, as well as fish from the nearby Yellow River—and, of course, turtles.

But Fu Hao did more than enjoy life. She was an extremely important person in the Shang dynasty. She commanded as many as 13,000 soldiers. She was also one of King Wu Ding's 64 wives—and his trusted advisor. Inscriptions on bronze items show us that the king had her conduct important ceremonies, including animal and human sacrifices, maybe using a stone axe found near her body

Radiocarbon Dating

All living things have a type of the chemical carbon known as carbon 14. This makes radiocarbon dating—a process used to tell the age of something that was once alive—possible. Carbon 14 is formed from nitrogen molecules in Earth's atmosphere. It combines with oxygen to form carbon dioxide, which is taken in by plants and used as food. People and animals get carbon 14 when they eat plants.

As carbon 14 ages, it decays and slowly turns back into nitrogen. Scientists know that it takes 5,730 years for half the

carbon 14 in the remains of a plant or animal to turn into nitrogen. By measuring how much of the radioactive carbon 14 has been lost in an artifact, archaeologists can determine how old the artifact is. That is, they can determine the age if it is less than 50,000 years old. The amount of carbon 14 in artifacts older than that is too small to measure.

When archaeologists found millet near a skeleton from the Shang dynasty, they used radiocarbon dating to confirm what contextual dating had led them to suspect: millet was used as food by Shang-dynasty people.

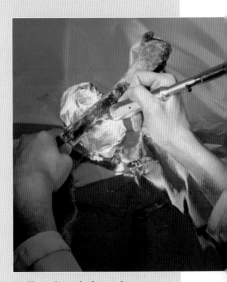

Radiocarbon dating a bone

with a human head surrounded by the heads of tigers.

A Window on Life Long Ago

What did the tomb tell us about the way the rich lived in Shang times? It's hard to be completely sure from just one example, but it certainly looks as if the rich had plenty of tasty food, beautiful clothes and jewelry,

and lots of servants. They had control over many people who were less fortunate than themselves and were responsible for important religious and military duties.

We should thank the turtle for telling its silent tales. But first we have to thank the archaeologists. Using the things Fu Hao was buried with, along with some oracle bones, they have opened a window into the past for all of us.

Meet an Archaeologist

Since 1997, Dr. Zhichun Jing of the University of British Columbia has been part of an international team working in Anyang, the last capital of the Shang dynasty.

◙ What new discoveries are you hoping to make in Anyang?

◙ Anyang has been excavated for many years. However, almost all the work had been on the Shang capital site itself. Now we are investigating sites across the Huan River, looking at settlement patterns over time and space. We are studying how human activities have had impacts on the environment, as well as how humans have reacted to environmental changes.

◙ Are there any newer techniques that have been particularly helpful to your own work?

◙ One of the new techniques we are using is high-resolution satellite imagery. But you can hardly find a discipline that has nothing to do with archaeology. It borrows methods from many different disciplines such as geology and zoology to solve archaeological mysteries and problems, such as population movement, agricultural origin, and detection of buried cities.

◙ What was the most important discovery you've ever made?

◙ I would say the Huanbei Shang city we located in 2001 was the most exciting discovery we have made. It is the largest Shang urban center

ever found, over 500 hectares [more than two square miles, about one-quarter the area of Manhattan]. This new city site will help us understand how the Shang society developed. It is important too because we made this discovery through our geoarchaeological drilling program instead of by accident. There are very few cases when large ancient settlements of the Early Bronze Age in China were not discovered by accident.

Believe it or not, for us it was much more exciting to detect pounded earth [which Shang buildings and city walls were made of] than to find bronzes or jades in a tomb.

∧ This elevated view shows a chariot with two human and two horse skeletons unearthed near Anyang.

◘ What are the biggest rewards in being an archaeologist?

▣ The biggest reward for me is to learn how to appreciate the diversity of world cultures and contribute our knowledge about the past to the understanding of where we came from, where we are, and where we go for the future [that] humans across the world will share. And we love to do fieldwork—you never know what will come to your eyes.

◘ What are the most significant challenges facing archaeologists working in China today?

▣ Economic development threatens our responsibilities for preserving cultural heritages. These cultural heritages belong to not only China but also the whole world.

◘ Central Asia has been called "an archaeologist's dream land" of potential discoveries. Would you say the same about China?

▣ I would even call China "an archaeologist's dream land" of mysteries. Discoveries in the past two decades have revealed civilizations that no one had ever expected. They have also transformed our basic understanding of Chinese civilization, which was traditionally believed to originate and center in the Central Plain (Yellow River). Today we know there were other cultures in other regions. More and more discoveries have shown that the development of early civilizations is totally different from what we have learned from traditional historical records. It seems that there are many mysteries waiting for archaeologists to solve.

◘ Do you have any advice for young people who want to become archaeologists?

▣ Doing archaeology is a lot of fun, but it is a scientific discipline that requires knowledge of many different subjects. If you want to be an archaeologist, my suggestion would be to get your hands dirty in the field and work very hard.

A Silent Army

How many soldiers are enough to guard an emperor in the afterlife?

I
t was 1974. In Xi'an (pronounced shee-an), 580 miles (930 km) southwest of Beijing, some farmers were digging a well. Reaching a level 15 feet (4.6 m) below ground, they uncovered a fragment of pottery that looked like the head of a very large sculpture of a man. The farmers could tell right away that this pottery was more important than finishing the well. They told a local official, who called

< The discovery of pits near the tomb of China's first emperor filled with hundreds of terra-cotta soldiers was one of the most amazing archaeological finds ever made.

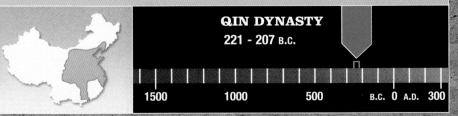

QIN DYNASTY
221 - 207 B.C.

1500   1000   500   B.C. 0 A.D. 300

∧ An archer lies in a partly excavated section of Pit 2. Other figures guarding Qin Shi Huangdi's tomb included cavalry troops, charioteers, and infantrymen.

in archaeologists right away. Working like crime scene investigators, the archaeologists carefully excavated the area around the farmers' well. They found many statues of soldiers made of a red clay called *terra-cotta*. They also found clay horses and chariots. It was as if a whole army lay beneath the earth. The site is only a mile from the main tomb of the First Emperor of China, Qin Shi Huangdi, who lived from 259 B.C. to 210 B.C. They knew this massive group of sculptures must be part of his tomb complex.

Over the next six years, the investigators detected three underground pits covering more than 200,000 square feet (22,000 meters sq.)—larger than the Louisiana Superdome. Ranged over this huge space were about 8,000 terra-cotta warriors and horses buried in tunnels or rooms that were separated by walls made of rammed earth. Some figures stood tall; others kneeled. Horses galloped or waited in harnesses.

How They Were Made

Each sculpture was life-size. Actually, the soldiers were even bigger than life. They stood about six feet (1.8 m) tall, which was taller than most Chinese people were at the time they were made. This would have made them seem especially strong and powerful. Each figure's face had a different expression, hairstyle, and clothing. Each one was marked with his army rank.

From studying the way the warriors were made, archaeologists concluded that Qin craftsman had an

∧ The figures of horses found in the pits were every bit as realistic and lifelike as the terra-cotta soldiers were.

extremely high level of technical skill. The various parts of the sculptures— legs, arms, bodies, fronts of heads, and backs of heads—were made in separate molds. Then each warrior was glued together.

Over the molded parts, craftsmen attached individually sculpted ears, noses, hair, and facial expressions, as well as military armor, belts, and other precise costume details. They then fired the completed sculpture in a pottery kiln and painted the finished product. As a result of such careful attention to detail, no two warriors, or horses, are exactly the same.

It appears that the craftsmen who made the sculptures were proud of their work. The name of the person who built each figure was found inscribed on the warrior's robe, leg, or armor.

< This life-size archer once held a real crossbow in his hands. Some experts consider him to be the best crafted of all the terra-cotta soldiers.

The First Emperor

The Qin dynasty ruled about 1,000 years later than Fu Hao's time. It was around this time that historians began to put together a written record of China's history. So we have more than turtle shells to help us interpret the terra-cotta warriors and understand the Emperor's life.

From the time he was a child, Ying Zheng planned ahead. When he inherited the throne of the Qin (pronounced chin) kingdom at age 13, he ordered workers to begin building his tomb. Then he got busy conquering the many neighboring kingdoms in the enormous plains around the Yellow River. Eventually Ying united the kingdoms into an empire. He took the name Qin Shi Huangdi, which means "First Emperor of Qin." Historians believe that the name Qin is the source of the word "China."

The Great Wall

Shi Huangdi's reign lasted 37 years. During much of that time, the dynasty was either at war or defending its borders from invaders. Under his rule, several sections of the defensive wall built over previous centuries were rebuilt, strengthened, connected, and extended into what we know today as the Great Wall of China.

> Although Qin Shi Huangdi's tomb has never been excavated, an artist has illustrated how the tomb might look, based on historical descriptions of the interior.

Preparing the Tomb

While the Great Wall was visible for many miles and remains an important symbol of China, Qin Shi Huangdi's tomb was even more amazing. Over the course of his reign, some 700,000 workers were involved in its construction. A historian of the time recorded that pearls were placed in the ceiling of his burial chamber to represent the stars. A map of the Qin empire, with its rivers and lakes filled with liquid mercury, was said to have been carved into the floor of the tomb. It is believed that the Emperor felt so strongly about keeping the details of the tomb's construction a secret that he had thousands of workers buried alive when the tomb was sealed.

Though archaeologists know the location of this tomb, they haven't yet found the entrance, and they must be very careful when they do find it because if it really contains rivers of mercury, it will be poisonous to anyone who enters.

It may come as no surprise that Qin Shi Huangdi was a feared and hated ruler. Perhaps he realized this and also planned on bringing protection with him to the afterlife. The emperor always thought big, so he brought not just some soldiers but an entire army.

The Terra-Cotta Army Today

Archaeologists are still digging up terra-cotta soldiers. In fact, in the 30 years since the army was discovered, only 1,000 of the estimated 8,000 soldiers have been uncovered. But the

terra-cotta army is also one of the most popular tourist destinations in China and is facing a dangerous modern enemy. In the 1990s the Chinese government erected enormous buildings over the dig site to protect the warriors from the weather and to allow visitors—1.5 million each year—to come and watch the ongoing excavation.

But the site is in Xi'an, which is one of the most polluted cities in the world. In addition, all those visitors breathing in a closed building have added a lot of moisture to the air. The moisture got so bad that mold has grown on many of the statues.

Though Qin Shi Huangdi clearly thought that 8,000 terra-cotta soldiers were enough to defend him in the afterlife, it doesn't look as if he considered who would defend those soldiers.

Ground-penetrating Radar

Ground-penetrating radar (GPR) is a special use of radar technology that helps to locate buried archaeological artifacts and features near the surface. Using antennae and a computer in a portable system, archaeologists collect and then process data to create an image of hidden structures and artifacts. GPR was used to estimate how many terra-cotta soldiers surround Qin Shi Huangdi's tomb, including those in pits that have not yet been excavated.

Conservationists (professionals who work to preserve important historical artifacts) are working now to figure out how to reduce the amount of damage pollution and visitors do to this ancient army so that they can continue to stand guard well into the future.

< A few of the soldiers still show their original paint. Technicians use the latest techniques to determine how the soldiers were painted.

<< Workers try to piece together one of the terra-cotta warriors found in Pit 1. Thousands of figures await eventual reconstruction.

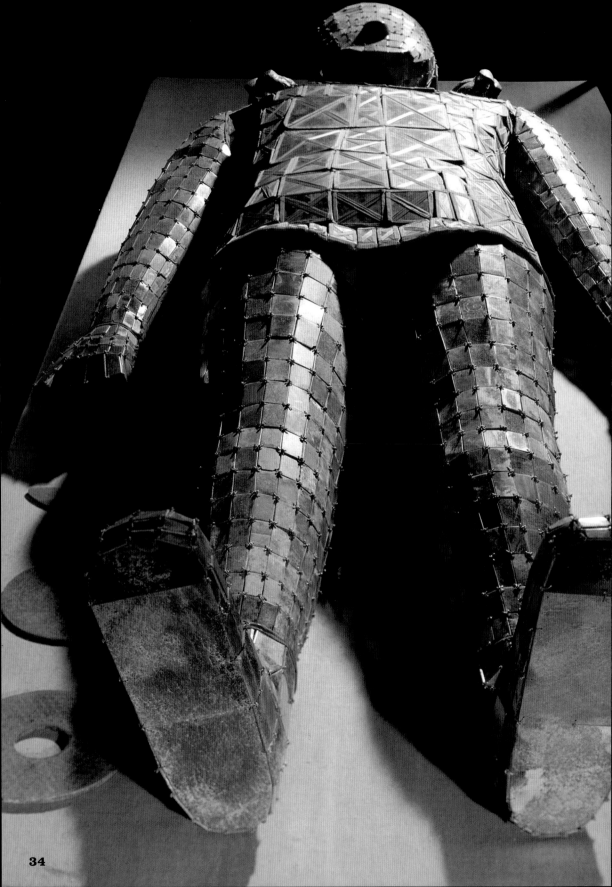

Dressed for Success

CHAPTER

4

How can archaeologists prove that stories of jade burial suits are true?

The ancient Chinese buried pieces of jade with dead rulers to protect the body and spirit. But a whole human-sized burial suit made entirely of jade? Despite stories, no one thought such an incredible garment existed—until Liu Sheng's tomb was discovered in Hebei province in 1968.

Liu Sheng was the son of the Han emperor Jing Di. He lived a luxurious life during the Han

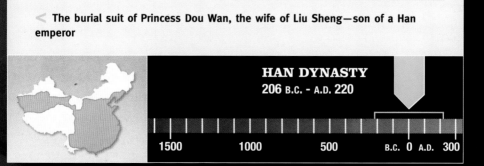

< The burial suit of Princess Dou Wan, the wife of Liu Sheng—son of a Han emperor

HAN DYNASTY
206 B.C. - A.D. 220

1500   1000   500   B.C. 0 A.D. 300

> Scientists are working to restore a jade head, part of a burial suit found in another royal tomb.

∨ A porcupine, crafted during the Han dynasty

dynasty, and his death was every bit as full of luxury. Clearly, Liu Sheng had every intention of taking the good life with him.

When Liu Sheng's tomb and his body were discovered, archaeologists could see that Chinese burial customs had changed yet again. Jade took on a new importance.

Inside Liu Sheng's Tomb

Liu Sheng and one of his wives, Dou Wan, were buried in caves hollowed out of a mountainside. Like Fu Hao,

Liu Sheng was buried with thousands of valuable objects. Like Emperor Qin Shi Huangdi, Liu Sheng was buried with stone figures, not real people. Human sacrifice had stopped being part of the burial ritual. And like members of the Chinese upper classes since the Neolithic age, he was buried with jade objects.

But Liu Sheng wasn't just buried with jade objects. Unlike any of these earlier rulers, Liu Sheng and his wife were buried in suits made entirely of pieces of jade. Archaeologists were astonished with their discovery.

The Jade Suits

The jade suits looked like a kind of
armor called lamellar armor—armor
made up of thousands of individual
pieces stiched together. The pieces
were made of jade. They were sewn
together with gold wire. Altogether,
there were 2,498 pieces of jade and
two and a half pounds of gold wire in
Liu's suit. There were different sections for the face, head, front, back,

> This jolly terra-cotta figure pounding a drum
is a singer-storyteller from the Han period.

arms, hands, legs, and feet. Arch-aeologists say Liu Sheng's and Dou Wan's suits each probably took ten years to make.

What was the point of suiting up in jade? Jade was hard and durable. It was thought to have magical powers to preserve the body and chase away evil spirits. Years before, it was common for people of the ruling class to be buried with jade pieces in their ears, eyes, and noses. But Liu Sheng's and Dou Wan's suits were the first full jade suits discovered. Since then archaeologists have found about a dozen more.

Archaeologists knew about jade suits from an early writing by Wei Hong (1st Century A.D.): "When the emperor died, a pearl was placed in his mouth: his body was wrapped around with twelve layers of reddish yellow silk. Jade was used to make the garment. It had the shape of armor and the jade pieces were stitched together with gold threads." But until they

▽ **Near the site of a royal Han tomb, visitors pay a fee to dig up replicas of ancient artifacts.**

∧ An artist weaves a silk tapestry using a traditional machine. Long an important part of their culture, the Chinese began trading silk with Europeans during the Han dynasty.

uncovered the tomb of Liu Sheng, no one had ever had proof that Wei Hong was right.

The Importance of Silk

Under the jade suit, Liu Sheng's body was wrapped in layers of silk. The Chinese had been raising silkworms for thousands of years to spin silk, but it was during the Han dynasty that travelers began coming from Europe, particularly the Roman Empire, to buy it. The right to wear it was reserved for nobles.

Regardless of rank, nobody was permitted to take silk-harvesting secrets from China. Silk was so valuable it was used as money. Chinese merchants were permitted to sell silk in other countries. However, anyone caught removing either silkworm eggs or cocoons from China was put to death.

More Secrets?

Liu Sheng's tomb was found in a cave. China has many mountains and many caves. Archaeologists will continue to search these places and others for more exciting discoveries.

∧ Unearthed from a royal tomb, this gilded silkworm promises fine clothing after death.

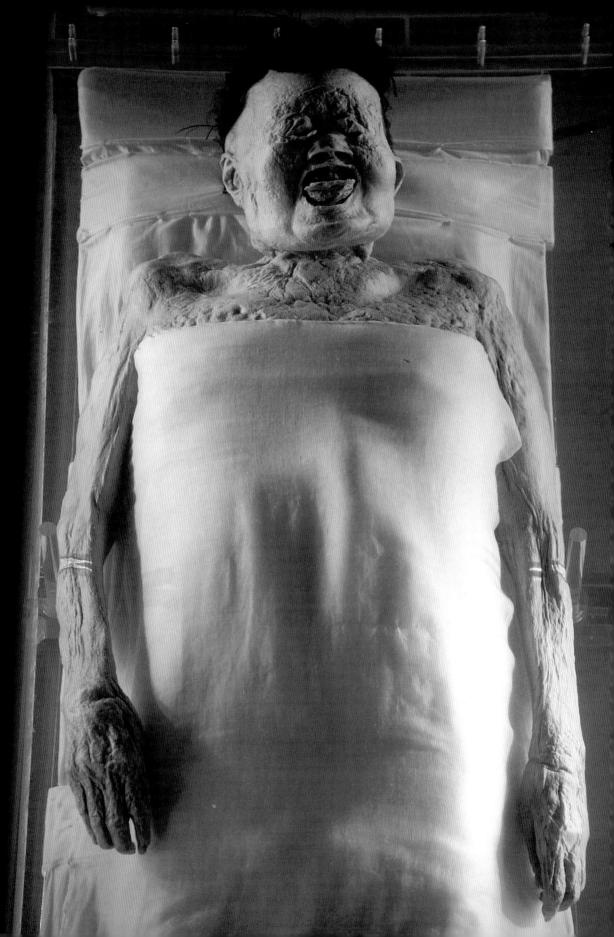

Learn from Your Mummy

CHAPTER 5

What can we learn from the best-preserved mummy in the world?

I n 1971, workers digging an air raid shelter near the city of Changsha in Hunan province uncovered an enormous tomb. Immediately they called in archaeologists. In time more than 1,000 artifacts were unearthed, including one incredible treasure: the best-preserved mummy in the world. Her name is Xin Zhui, and she is known as Lady Dai.

< Scientists have learned much from their examination of the amazing mummy of Lady Dai.

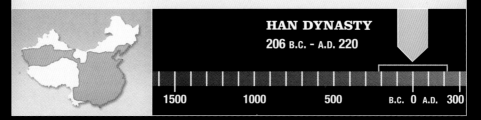

HAN DYNASTY
206 B.C. - A.D. 220

1500   1000   500   B.C. 0 A.D. 300

Modern technology has helped to reveal the secrets of Lady Dai's mummy. Scientists were able to discover what caused her death 2,000 years ago.

Lady Dai

Xin Zhui was the wife of an important ruler in the Han dynasty. Her husband was the Chancellor of the Kingdom of Changsha and Marquis of Dai. Lady Dai died between 168 B.C. and 165 B.C., when she was about 50 years old. The contents of her tomb point to a wealthy, important woman who liked to eat. Along with lacquer dinnerware and fine fabrics, there were chests containing fruit, pigs, oxen, pheasant, soybeans, and other foods.

Everything inside Lady Dai's tomb was exceptionally well preserved, including the lady herself. Her skin was soft. She had a full head of hair. Her arms and legs could be moved easily.

The Autopsy

In fact, Lady Dai was so well preserved that scientists were able to do an autopsy—a surgical procedure in which internal organs are removed and studied to find a cause of death. Autopsies are done today all the time—but not on 2,000-year-old corpses.

Inside Lady Dai, scientists found more surprises. There were melon seeds in her stomach. Red blood filled

< This historical reconstruction shows Lady Dai as she might have looked. She was 5 feet, 2 inches (158 cm) tall and was thought to be a great beauty in her day.

The Tomb of Lady Dai

It took four months for archaeologists to dig their way to the bottom of the funnel-shaped pit that formed Lady Di's grave. About 52 feet (16 m) down, atop a carpet of 26 bamboo mats, there was an enormous wooden box. Inside was a treasure trove of grave goods—items meant for the use of the deceased in the afterlife. These goods surrounded a series of plain coffins and ornate caskets, one inside the other. Five tons of charcoal covered the wooden box, meant to absorb any wetness that might make its way through a layer of white clay between two and four feet (0.6 to 1.2 m) thick.

At the center of it all was the richest prize the archaeologists could have imagined—the best pre-served mummy in the world, Lady Dai. (It should be said that Lady Dai was not a mummy in the usual sense of the word. Her body was not prepared using the traditional mummification steps well known from ancient Egypt. In the case of Lady Dai, her corpse was splendidly preserved because of the environmental conditions of her burial.)

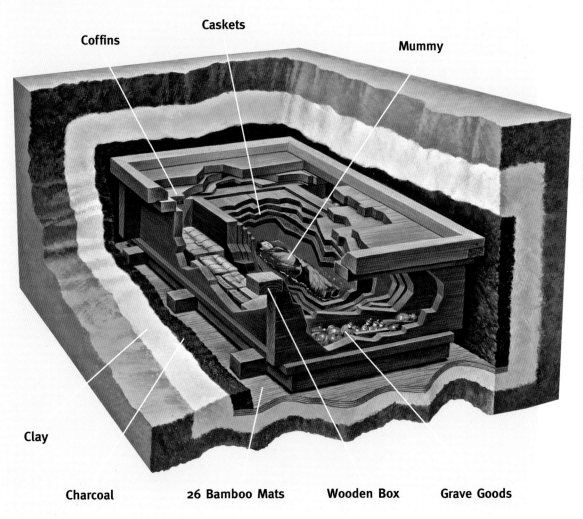

Coffins

Caskets

Mummy

Clay

Charcoal   26 Bamboo Mats   Wooden Box   Grave Goods

Desert Mummies

Remarkably well-preserved corpses have been found elsewhere in China as well. A group of mummies more than 2,000 years old were found in western China's Takla Makan Desert. The bodies have been preserved by the dry desert conditions and the high amount of salt in the earth.

These mummies are especially mysterious because their light-colored hair, facial features, and clothing all make archaeologists think they may have been part of an ancient culture that lived where Central Asia and China came into contact. This would seem to show that the two worlds were exchanging goods and ideas many years before the famous Silk Road linked China and the Middle East. There may have been a number of these cultures, but the so-called Desert Mummies of the Tarim Basin are still mostly a mystery.

∧ This extraordinary mummy of a woman was unearthed from the desert sand. She had long brown-blond hair and wore a felt hat trimmed with a goose feather.

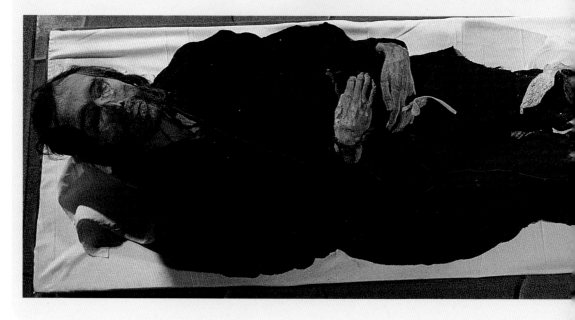

A mummified infant boy was also found. He was wrapped in woolen cloth, and a smooth stone covered each of his eyes.

These mummified remains are those of a man about 55 years old. He wore a red woolen bracelet on his right wrist and deerskin boots on his feet.

her veins. Her liver, lungs, and other organs were perfectly preserved. Her brain was in one piece, although it had shrunk. Scientists found she had blockages of her bile ducts, a parasite, and hardening of the arteries. But none of these conditions killed her. She died of a heart attack, probably brought on by too much rich food and too little exercise.

Preserving Lady Dai

Why did Lady Dai's body last so well for so long? Nobody knows for sure. It could be the mysterious reddish liquid in which she was found immersed. Tests showed the liquid contained salt and the chemical magnesium, but scientists are still trying to identify the other ingredients.

There could be other reasons. Her body was wrapped in 20 layers of silk, which could have kept out flesh-eating bacteria. It was inside four coffins, which were covered with five tons of charcoal. Charcoal is known to prevent spoilage and keep away bacteria.

The Search Continues

China's tombs and mummies have been a tremendous source of information for archaeologists. And archaeologists never know when a new discovery will be made, a discovery perhaps richer than anything they've found in the past.

Good Job, Goodbye!

CHAPTER 6

Is the story of the past the same for both the rich and the poor?

Fu Hao and Shi Huangdi were remarkable people. Fu Hao was a woman military leader, and Shi Huangdi was a mighty emperor who unified China. But they were also lucky. They, and Liu Sheng too, were born members of rich, powerful ruling classes. All that money and power allowed them to build the incredible tombs from which archaeologists have learned so much. Few people at any time or in any place have been as rich and powerful as these.

< A girl watches archaeologists excavating the foundations of the largest building ever discovered from the Shang dynasty at the Huanbei Shang city in Anyang.

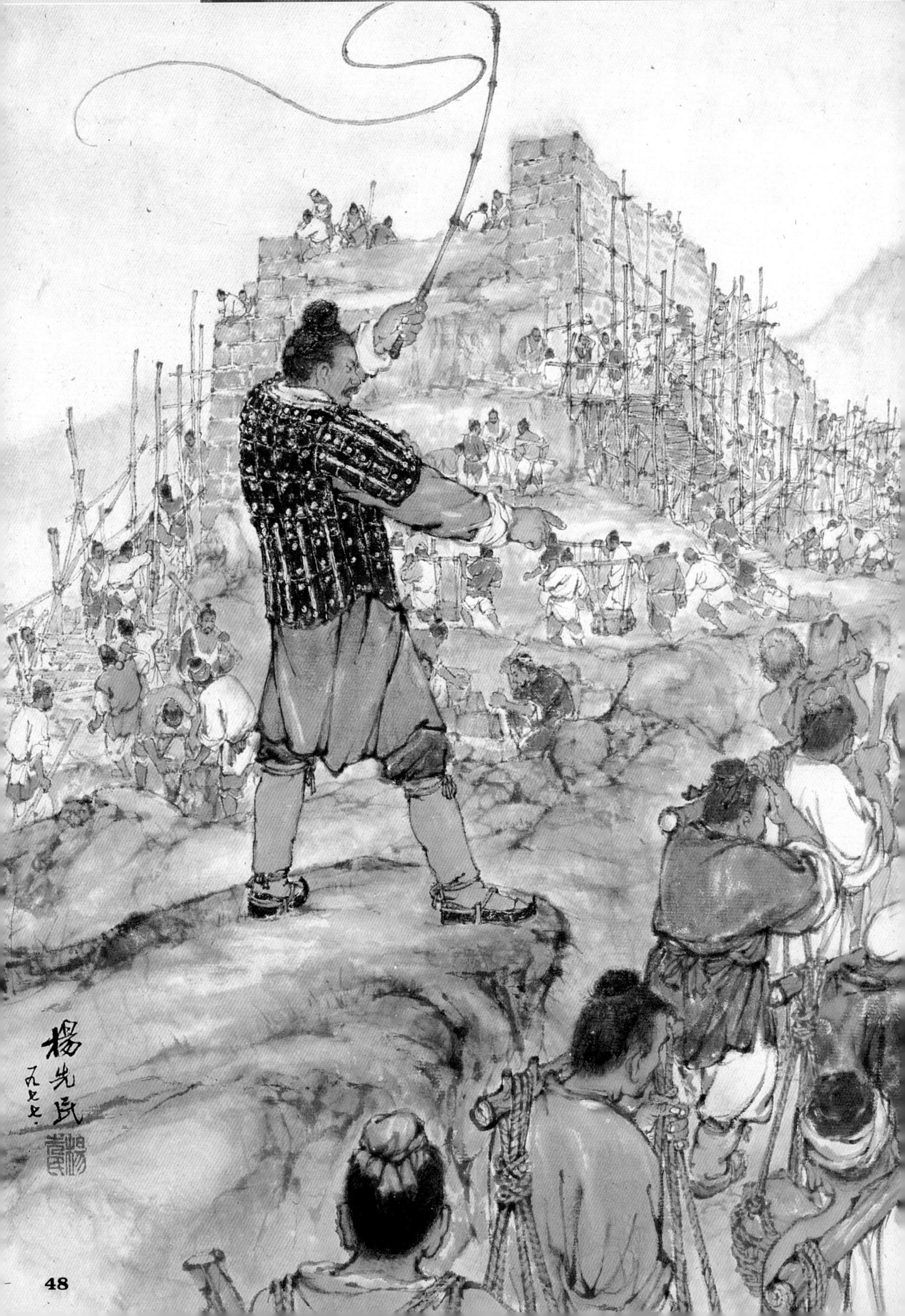

∧ Using historically authentic methods, modern workers create a rammed-earth wall. Walls and foundations built in this way have lasted for thousands of years.

In all of the periods of ancient China, the vast majority of people were peasants who worked the land, workers who built the great cities and tombs, merchants who bought and sold goods, and craftworkers who created the clothing, jewelry, food containers, statues, and the many other manufactured goods needed by rich and poor alike. Luckily for us, the rich could not have lived their lives or built their tombs without the contributions of thousands of ordinary people. Archaeologists use evidence found in the tombs of rulers to figure out how their subjects lived.

< The emperor Qin Shi Huangdi sent 700,000 forced laborers to build his Great Wall.

Royal Tomb Builders

The workers who built the royal tombs were slaves, convicts, or prisoners taken in war and forced to labor for their captors. These workers might hold the same job for their whole lives, because tombs, walls, and other construction projects could take 30 or 40 years to build.

Even if the tomb builders lived to finish the job, they couldn't count on a vacation. In Shang times, when construction projects were completed, humans and animals were often sacrificed to the gods. Even much later in the Qin dynasty, many thousands of workers were killed to protect the king's secrets.

Servants

From the many tombs that have now been discovered and excavated, and from writings of the time, archaeologists have been able to put together a picture of certain aspects of the belief in an afterlife as shown by some burial rituals in ancient China. The ancient Chinese believed that the afterlife was an extension of life on Earth. A ruler's tomb was his or her palace in death. Inside the tomb, the dead ruler was expected to have feasts and carry out the same religious rituals the live one had. Of course, they would need their servants to do the cooking, cleaning, and waiting that they had done so well in life. So, when a ruler died, the ruler's personal servants were often killed, too, in order to serve their masters in the afterlife. This practice was called "following in death" and was common in many ancient cultures. It was more common during the Shang dynasty and in earlier times. By the time of the Qin dynasty, figurines of servants had replaced the real thing.

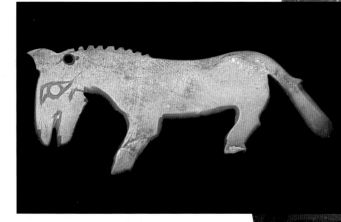

∧ This jade carving of a horse dates to the Bronze Age period of the Shang dynasty.

> People of the Neolithic period Yangshao culture created this water flask, or ping.

Craftworkers

In order to live a sumptuous life in the spirit world, rulers made sure that their tombs were stocked with food and wine, all packed in beautiful containers. They also needed religious vessels—vases and jars and bowls to be used in ceremonies—and other everyday manufactured items, such as clothing, lamps, and furniture. And they needed the special jade pieces that they believed would keep them immortal. From examining these grave goods, archaeologists have learned a lot about the techniques used by craftworkers in ancient China.

The Earliest Artisans

Back in the Neolithic age, as many as 10,000 years ago, early craftworkers made beautiful vessels from clay. One Neolithic culture, the Longshan, used clay from the Yellow River to make delicate black pottery. The pottery was baked in kilns. The firing process gives the pottery its black color.

The artisans' kilns were so hot they could melt metal. These ovens would come in handy in later cultures, when craftsmen began to use bronze.

A Bell Nobody Will Ever Ring

In 1985, archaeologists found a tiny jade bell. At only one inch (2.5 cm) high, the bell was so small it can't ever be rung. The bell is one of nearly 1,000 carved jade pieces found at Lingjiatan, along with pottery and stoneware. They also found the remains of a city more than 5,500 years old, a thousand years older than any other discovered so far in China.

< A painted vessel shows the artistic skill of the Yangshao people.

∧ This jade ritual blade, called a zhang, was found at Erlitou.
Such blades are incredibly thin and can be up to three feet (0.9 m) long.

Neolithic finds like this one are very important because in spite of the lack of written texts, archaeologists can study the artifacts and the site layout to piece together many aspects of ancient life.

An amazing thing that archaeologists discovered is that these Neolithic jade workers used quite advanced technology. Archaeologist Zhang Jingguo, who is supervising the ongoing excavation, says that the jade objects show the artists knew some fancy carving techniques. Jade is an exceptionally hard mineral that can only be carved by using even harder substances, such as quartz sand or (in later times) diamond. The Lingjiatan artisans made special drills that not only were strong enough to carve with but also made straight holes, even when they were spinning at high speeds. To do this, members of this ancient culture had to know high-level science and math.

And Then Comes Bronze

In the Shang dynasty (the time of Fu Hao), most of the ritual vessels were made of bronze, a metal that is a mixture of copper, tin, and lead. The making of bronze arose around the world at different times. Archaeologists call the time a culture used bronze as its main metal that culture's Bronze Age. In ancient China, the Bronze Age falls between around 2000 B.C. and 400 B.C. The earliest major use of bronze in China found so far comes from Erlitou, in the city of Yanshi, south of the Yellow River. Many Chinese historians and archaeologists believe Erlitou was the capital of the Xia culture, which overlapped with the beginning of the Shang dynasty. Bronze items were mostly used as weapons like spearheads, arrowheads, and axes, or ceremonial vessels. Lower classes worked at making bronze items, but rarely used them.

∧ During the Shang dynasty, a bronze ding like this one would be used to cook for one's ancestors.

> This unusual Bronze Age sculpture of a greatly exaggerated face with horns is from the Shang period.

Even though most archaeological finds are from the tombs of the rich, archaeologists can see that life was very different for people from different parts of society. The cultures that we call ancient China were complex, with as many different ways of life as there are in modern cultures. As more discoveries are made, archaeologists will continue to explore all layers of these societies.

Tomb Robbers!

CHAPTER 7

What could be the harm in stealing things from the past?

People who built ancient tombs knew that the riches inside would be tempting to robbers. That's why Emperor Qin Shi Huangdi reportedly rigged his tomb with crossbows that would automatically shoot anybody entering it. Qin Shi Huangdi's tomb has not been opened in modern times, but archaeologists think it is likely that the tomb was looted in earlier times, despite Qin Shi Huangdi's precautions.

< Stolen from a tomb in northern China in 1994, this rare marble sculpture was returned to China in 2001 by the United States Customs Service. The artifact was seized prior to being offered at auction.

∧ Archaeologists excavate one of 24 pits leading to the tomb of Jing Di, fifth emperor of the Han dynasty.

Grave Robbing

Grave robbing is a problem that links modern China with its ancient past. Looters plunder ancient tombs and other sites to obtain artifacts. These are then sold to dealers and collectors around the world. They destroy the sites as well as the precious scientific information that the sites contain. Recently, within one five-year period, more than 220,000 ancient Chinese tombs were looted. Some experts estimate that nine out of ten of all the artifacts being sold today reached the market as the result of tomb robbing. Modern-day Chinese citizens can make money raiding tombs. In 2001 an antiquities dealer offered people near Xi'an $60 for a one-night theft. It would take some Chinese workers a year to earn $60. The dealers stand to make much, much more. Some looted bronzes have sold for as much as several million dollars on the international market!

Recovering the Goods

One target was the tomb of Empress Dou, who died in 135 B.C. Archaeologists think her tomb had been looted because the gold and silver artifacts buried with her were gone. But art dealers spread the word that collectors would still pay a lot for pots, statues, and other items.

Six statuettes stolen from

∧ **Another pit in Jing Di's tomb complex, which has been excavated since 1990. Sites such as this must be protected from tomb robbers in order to preserve China's ancient record.**

Empress Dou's tomb that were going to be sold in New York City were returned to China. They still had the tags from the auction house on them.

Penalties for Robbers

The Chinese government is working hard to stop the tomb robberies. Tomb robbers who are caught face severe punishment—even execution. Sometimes grave robbers create their own punishment. In 2004, three robbers were killed when a tomb they had broken into collapsed on them.

Even when robbers don't kill themselves, they do more damage than just stealing. Some blow up tomb entrances. Others rip up sites by digging with crude shovels. These methods ruin items that are important clues to ancient life, even if they're not worth a lot of money on the open market.

For instance, a grave robber who finds a bowl with preserved food inside might take just the bowl. But archaeologists could have learned things from the food, too, such as whether it was used for ordinary meals or for rituals. Also, archaeologists carefully note where everything in a site is located. If robbers move things, more than just relics are lost: Knowledge is lost as well.

∧ With the burial mound of Jing Di in the background, a farmer poses with his grandson, forming a splendid portrait of the links between China's past, present, and future.

Despite the problem of tomb robbers, the years ahead could reveal astonishing new finds. The field of archaeology is relatively new in China. New discoveries are being made all the time, whether through careful study or by happy accident. As one archaeologist says, "What's ahead? I believe that in the next 100 years, the land of Central Asia will become an archaeologist's dream land."

Glossary

antiquities – ancient relics

artifact – any object changed by human activity

Bronze Age – the time when a culture uses bronze as its main metal

carbon 14 – a form of the element carbon, found in all living things

circa – about; used to indicate a date that is approximate, and abbreviated as ca.

conservationists – persons dedicated to protecting natural resources and the environment

contextual dating – estimating the age of items from an unknown period by studying nearby items that had been linked to a specific period

ground-penetrating radar (GPR) – a special kind of radar technology, used to locate objects beneath the surface of the Earth

kiln – oven used to bake clay into pottery

lacquer – the sap of the ancient lac tree, used to waterproof bamboo and wood. It is used to produce everything from armor to chariots to coffins to boxes and cups.

lamellar armor – the most common type of armor in the ancient world, made up of individual pieces stitched together

Neolithic – the latest period of the Stone Age, when people used polished stone tools, domesticated plants and animals, made pottery, and lived in settled villages

oracle bones – turtle shells or oxen shoulder blades containing predictions of the future believed to have been made by gods

radiocarbon dating – a process in which scientists measure the amount of the chemical carbon 14 to determine the age of an artifact

rammed earth – a building process in which earth is pounded down so hard it compresses into a rocklike hardness

rituals – formal ceremonies, often religious

terra-cotta – hardened red clay

vessels – containers, jars, and bowls for rituals or everyday use

∧ Ancient Chinese script on the hem of one of the terra-cotta soldiers says "Property of the Royal Household."

Bibliography

Books

Morton, W. Scott, and Charlton M. Lewis. *China: Its History and Culture.* 4th edition. New York: McGraw-Hill, 2005.

Roberts, J. A. G. *A Concise History of China.* Cambridge: Harvard University Press, 1999.

Shaughnessy, Edward L., ed. *China: Empire and Civilization.* New York: Oxford University Press, 2005.

Articles

"Chinese Lady Dai Leaves Egyptian Mummies for Dead." www.chinadaily .com.cn, August 25, 2004.

"New Finds Unearth Early Chinese History." *China Daily*, January 13, 2005.

"Pipeline Project Uncovers 18 Archaeological Sites." www.chinadaily .com.cn, February 4, 2003.

"7,000-year-old Relics Unearthed in Northwest China." *People's Daily*, October 15, 2002.

"7,000-year-old Village Found in Ningbo." www.chinadaily.com.cn, January 25, 2004.

"The Takla Makan Mummies." www.pbs.org/wgbh/nova, October 2000.

"Two Prehistoric City Sites Discovered in China." www.stonepages.com, November 3, 2004.

Further Reading and Information

Cotterel, Arthur. *Eyewitness: Ancient China.* New York: DK Children, 2000.

Kleeman, Terry, and Tracy Barrett. *The Ancient Chinese World.* New York: Oxford University Press, 2005.

Williams, Brian. *Ancient China* (See through History Series). New York: Viking Books, 1996.

Web Sites

www.nga.gov (National Gallery of Art)

www.historyforkids.org

Contains Chinese history, with a timeline; maps; articles about food, clothing, people, art, and architecture; and crafts and projects.

www.ancientchina.co.uk

The Web site of the British Museum offers virtual tours of ancient Chinese workshops, tombs, and villages.

∧ The back of a richly decorated bronze mirror from the Han dynasty

Index

Boldface indicates illustrations.

Afterlife
    beliefs about 50–51
Anyang area
    archaeologists in 24–25, **24, 25**
    building site **46–47**
    cemetery in **18–19**
    oracle bones from 22
Archaeological sites
    accidental discoveries 24,
        27–28, 41
    choosing 14, 16
    contextual dating 21, 22
    ground-penetrating radar 17,
        33
    map 9
    soil samples **12–13, 14–15**
    visitors digging at **38**
    water in 14, 20
    see also Tombs
Archaeologists
    definition 14
    hope for future finds 58
    introduction to 24–25
    tools 16–17, 23, 24, 33
Artifacts
    conservation of 33
    dating 21, 22, 23
    definition 14
    information from 52
    robbing tombs for 20, 55–57
Artisans 51
Assassination attempt **16–17**
Autopsies 42, 43

Bronze Age 52–53
    see also Shang dynasty
Bronze objects
    animal decoration **63**
    creation of 52
    horse **4**
    human figure **8**
    mirror **60**
    vessels **20, 53**
Buildings
    rammed-earth walls 28, 49
    Shang dynasty **46–47**

Cemetery **18–19**
    see also Tombs
Changsha (city)
    tomb near 41
Charcoal 43, 45
Chariots **25, 28**

Children
    mummy of **45**
China
    economic development 25
    grave robbing and penalties in
        56–57
    silk production as state secret
        of 39
    source of word 30
Chinese Academy of Social
    Sciences 29
Chinese script 29, **59**
Coffins **43**, 45
Conservationists
    definition 33
Cowry shells 20
Craftworkers 51

Desert
    mummies 44–45, **44–45**
Di, Jing
    son of 35
    tomb **56, 57, 58**
Ding
    definition 22
Ding, Wu 22
Dogs 20

Erlitou area
    bronze usage in 52
    jade ritual blade from **52**

"Following in death"
    beliefs about 50
Foods 42, 51

Gong
    definition **22**
Great Wall of China **6, 48**
    construction 30
    symbolism 32

Han dynasty
    archaeological excavations 56,
        57
    bronze decoration **63**
    incense burner **15**
    jade burial suits 14, **34–35, 37**
        35–37, 38
    maps 35, 41
    mirror **60**
    sculptures **4, 36**
    silk trade 39
    terra-cotta figure **37**
    timeline 11, 17

Hao, Fu
    life of 22–23, 46
    oracle bones about 22
    tomb 14
Helmet **11**
History
    changing views of 25
    sources 13–17
    timeline 10–11, 17
Hong, Wei 38–39
Horses
    sculptures **4, 28, 29, 50**
    skeletons 25
Huanbei Shang city
    building site **46–47**
Huangdi, Qin Shi
    illustrations **16–17, 48**
    reign 30, 32
    terra-cotta figures guarding
        26–27, 28, **28, 29,**
        30–31, 32
    tomb complex **11, 12–13,**
        30–31, 32, 55
    wealth 46
Human sacrifice 22–23, 36, 49,
    50

Incense burner **15**

Jade burial suits
    construction 37–38
    examples 14, **34–37**
    magical properties 35, 38
Jade objects
    bell 51–52
    horse **50**
    ritual blade (zhang) **52**
Jing, Zhichun 24–25, **24**
Jingguo, Zhang 52

Laboring classes
    artisans and craftworkers 51
    bronze work 52
    Great Wall built by 48
    servants 50
    tombs built by 49
Lady Dai
    see Zhui, Xin (Lady Dai)
Lingjiatan (city)
    jade pieces of 51–52
Longshan culture 51

Maps
    archaeological sites 9
    Han dynasty 35, 41

Qin dynasty 27
Shang dynasty 19
in tomb 32
Mercury
in tomb 32
Military
equipment 11
leaders 22ñ23
terra-cotta figures of 26–29,
32–33, 59
Millet 21, 22
Mirror 60
Mummies
autopsies of 42, 44
desert areas 44–45
Lady Dai 40
preservation 43, 45
Murowchick, Robert 8, 9

Neolithic culture
archaeological site 9
artisans 51
jade objects 51–52
timeline 10
vessels 50, 51

Oracle
definition 21
Oracle bones
uses of 21, 21–22
Oral tradition 13–14
Ox bones
uses of 21, 21–22

Pearls 32, 38
Ping
definition 50
Porcupine sculpture 36
Pottery
Longshan culture 51
see also Terra-cotta figures

Qin dynasty
beliefs about afterlife 50
Great Wall in 30
map 27
terra-cotta figures 26–27,
28–33, 28, 29, 30–31,
32
timeline 10, 17
workers in 49

Radar technology
ground-penetrating 17, 33
Radiocarbon dating 23
Ritual objects
incense burner 15
jade blade (zhang) 52

oracle bones 21, 21–22
Ruling classes
wealth 22–23, 46

Satellite imagery 24
Sculpture
bronze head 20, 53
horses 4, 28, 29, 50
human figures 8, 11
marble 54–55
porcupine 36
terra-cotta soldiers 26–27,
28–33, 28, 29, 30–31,
32
tiger 10
Servants 50
Shamans 21–22
Shang dynasty
beliefs about afterlife 50
bronze usage in 52–53
building site 46–47
map 19
ruling class 22–23
sculptures 8, 10, 20, 50, 53
timeline 10, 17
tombs 18–19, 20–21
urban center 24
vessels and containers 20, 22,
53
workers in 49
Sheng, Liu
jade burial suit 14, 37–39
reign 35–36
tomb 36, 39
wealth 46
Silk
in burials 38, 39, 45
importance 39
tapestry 39

Takla Makan Desert
mummies 44
Tarim Basin
mummies 44
Technology
ground-penetrating radar 17,
33
radiocarbon dating 23
satellite imagery 24
for working jade 52
Terra-cotta figures
creation of 28–29
definition 28
drummer 37
head 11
script on 29, 59
soldiers 26–27, 28–33, 28, 29,
30–31, 32

Tiger sculpture 10
Timeline 10–11
Tomb robbers 20, 55–57
Tombs
construction 28, 43, 45, 49
example of contents 20–21
excavations 18–19, 56, 57
information from 19
jade burial suits 14, 34–38
mercury in 32
protection of 55
role in afterlife 50–51
silk in 38, 39, 45
terra-cotta soldiers guarding
26–27, 28–33, 28, 29,
30–31, 32
Tourists 33, 38
Turtle shells 19, 21, 21–22

United States Custom Service 55

Vessels and containers
bronze 20, 53
ding, for cooking 53
gong, for wine 22
painted 51
ping, for water 50

Walls
rammed-earth 28, 49
Wan, Dou
jade burial suit 34–35, 38
tomb 36, 56–57
Weaving 39
Women
military leaders 22–23
mummies 40, 44

Xia culture 52
Xi'an (city)
pollution 33

Yangshao culture 50, 51
Yanshi (city)
bronze usage in 52
Yellow River 30, 51

Zhang
definition 52
Zheng, Ying 30
Zhenxiang, Zheng 20–21
Zhui, Xin (Lady Dai)
autopsy 42, 44
historical reconstruction 42
mummy 40–41
tomb 42, 43

About the Authors

JACQUELINE BALL is the award-winning author and producer of more than 100 books for children and young adults, including the *Dino School* series and *Step Back Science*.

RICHARD LEVEY is a business reporter and weekly columnist. His first children's book, *Dust Bowl! The 1930s Black Blizzard,* was published in 2005.

This is their first book for National Geographic.

Consultant

ROBERT MUROWCHICK is director of the International Center for East Asian Archaeology and Cultural History at Boston University, where he also serves as research associate professor of archaeology and anthropology. He earned his B.A. in archaeology from Yale College and his M.A. in regional studies–East Asia and his Ph.D. in anthropology from Harvard University. Dr. Murowchick frequently travels to China on archaeological research trips.

∧ A bronze decoration showing a wild animal biting a bird, from the Han period

One of the world's largest nonprofit scientific and educational organizations, the
National Geographic Society was founded
in 1888 "for the increase and diffusion of
geographic knowledge." Fulfilling this mission, the
Society educates and inspires millions every day
through its magazines, books, television programs,
videos, maps and atlases, research grants, the
National Geographic Bee, teacher workshops, and
innovative classroom materials. The Society is sup-
ported through membership dues, charitable gifts,
and income from the sale of its educational prod-
ucts. This support is vital to National Geographic's
mission to increase global understanding and pro-
mote conservation of our planet through explo-
ration, research, and education.

For more information, please call 1-800-NGS-LINE
(647-5463) or write to the following address:

National Geographic Society
1145 17th Street N.W.
Washington, D.C. 20036-4688
U.S.A.

Visit the Society's Web site:
www.nationalgeographic.com

Library of Congress Cataloging-in-Publication Data
available upon request
Hardcover ISBN-10: 0-7922-7783-X
          ISBN-13: 978-0-7922-7783-5
Library Edition ISBN-10: 0-7922-7856-9
          ISBN-13: 978-0-7922-7856-6

Printed in China

Book design by Dan Banks, Project Design Company
The body text is set in Century Schoolbook
The display text is set in Helvetica Neue, Clarendon

National Geographic Society

John M. Fahey, Jr., *President and Chief Executive
Officer;* Gilbert M. Grosvenor, *Chairman of the
Board;* Nina D. Hoffman, Executive Vice President,
President of Books and Education Publishing Group

National Geographic Children's Books and Education Publishing Group

Stephen Mico, *Executive Vice President and
Publisher of Children's Books and Education
Publishing Group*
Bea Jackson, *Design Director, Children's Books and
Education Publishing Group*
Margaret Sidlosky, *Illustrations Director, Children's
Books and Education Publishing Group*

Staff for This Book

Nancy Laties Feresten, *Vice President, Editor-in-
Chief of Children's Books*
Virginia Ann Koeth, *Project Editor*
Jim Hiscott, *Art Director*
National Geographic Image Sales, Jean Cantu, Lori
Epstein, *Illustrations Editors*
Carl Mehler, *Director of Maps*
Priyanka Lamichhane, *Editorial Assistant*
Margie Towery, *Indexer*
Rebecca Hinds, *Managing Editor*
R. Gary Colbert, *Production Director*
Lewis R. Bassford, *Production Manager*
Vincent P. Ryan, Maryclare Tracy, *Manufacturing
Managers*

Photo Credits

Front cover: O. Louis Mazzatenta
Spine: Raymond Gehman
Back cover: Background image: gds/sefa/Corbis;
Figure: O. Louis Mazzatenta

All images, except as noted below, are by O. Louis
Mazzatenta. 2-3, © Frank Krahmer/zefa/Corbis; 5,
© gds/ zefa/Corbis; 7, © gds/zefa/Corbis; 6,
Raymond Gehman/ National Geographic Image
Collection; 9, Courtesy of David J. Cohen; 16-17,
Painting by Yang Hsien-Min; 21 top, © Richard
Hamilton Smith/Corbis; 23, James King-Holmes/
Photo Researchers, Inc.; 24, Courtesy of Dr. Zhichun
Jing; 30-31, Yang Hsien-Min; 34, Erich Lessing/Art
Resource, NY; 40, Courtesy of Hunan Provincial
Museum, China; 42, Courtesy of Hunan Provincial
Museum, China; 43, Davis Meltzer; 44-45, Reza; 48,
Yang Hsien-Min; 49, Michael Yamashita; 51, ©
Bowers Museum of Cultural Art/Corbis; 52, The
Granger Collection, NY; 54-55, © Reuters/Corbis.

Front cover: A terra-cotta soldier from the tomb
complex of Qin Shi Huangdi
Page 1 and back cover: Part tiger, part human, a
marble monster from the Shang dynasty bares its
teeth.
Pages 2–3: A pine tree in the Huangshan
Mountains (Yellow Mountains), one of China's most
popular tourist attractions